Fisher-Price®

Ready Readers

Stage 1 Preschool

Copyright ©2002 by Modern Publishing, a division of Unisystems, Inc.
Fisher-Price and related trademarks, copyrights and character designs are used under license from Fisher-Price, Inc., a subsidiary of Mattel, Inc., East Aurora, NY 14052 U.S.A. ©2002 Mattel, Inc.
All Rights Reserved.

PRINTED IN THE U.S.A.

Manufactured for and distributed by Modern Publishing,
a division of Unisystems, Inc., New York, New York 10022

All text and art copyright ©2002 Modern Publishing,
a division of Unisystems, Inc., New York, New York 10022
All Rights Reserved.

™Ready Readers is a trademark owned by Modern Publishing, a division of Unisystems, Inc.
All Rights Reserved.

®Honey Bear Books is a trademark owned by Honey Bear Productions, Inc.,
and is registered in the U.S. Patent and Trademark Office.
All Rights Reserved.
No part of this book may be reproduced or copied in any
format without written permission of the publisher.

Printed in the U.S.A.
Series UPC: 11830

Dear Parents/Caregivers:

Children learn to read in stages, and all children develop reading skills at different ages. **Ready Readers™** were created to encourage children's interest in reading and to increase their reading skills. **Ready Readers™** stories are written on two levels to accommodate children ranging in grade level from preschool through third grade. These stages are meant to be used only as a guide.

Stage 1: Preschool—Grade 1

Stage 1 stories have short, simple sentences with large type. They are perfect for children who are getting ready to read or are just becoming familiar with reading on their own.

Stage 2: Grades 1—3

Stage 2 stories have longer sentences and are a bit more complex. They are suitable for children who are able to read but still may need help.

All of the **Ready Readers™** stories are fun, easy-to-follow tales that are colorfully illustrated. The stories are arranged in a progressive order of difficulty. Children should read the stories in order to move from the simplest vocabulary and concepts to the most difficult within each stage. Reading will become an exciting adventure. Soon your child will not only be ready, but eager to read.

Educational Consultant: Wendy Gelsanliter, M.S. in Early Childhood Education, Bank Street College of Education

Contents

Sherman Came for a Visit 5
When I Am Happy 35
Treasure Hunting at Tulip Park 65
No More Chores! 95
Colors for Me and You 125
Ed Can Help 155
Look at Lisa Go 185
Goldi's Locks 215
My Friend Nelly 245
Sara's Secret Hiding Place 275

Sherman Came for a Visit

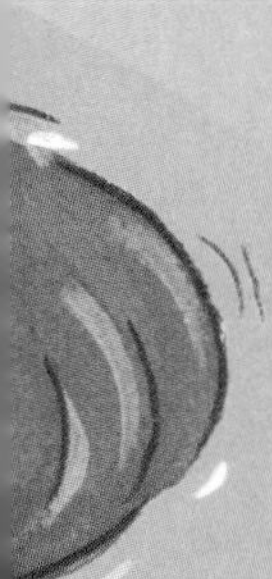

Written by Susan Kochan

Illustrated by Dudley Moseley

Here is my aunt Maybelle.
Here is Sherman, her dog.

When they came to visit,
Mom wished he was a frog.

Sherman is big and hairy.

Sherman likes to jump.

When Sherman got tired,
He laid down like a lump.

My brother tried to ride him.

Sherman hated that.

My sister tried to dress him.

He quickly ate her hat.

When dad tried to take a nap,

Sherman woke him up.

And when I tried to drink my juice,

Sherman took my cup.

I think he likes the baby.
Sherman licked her toes.

She reached out her fingers
to pet him on the nose.

Sherman got excited
when someone knocked
on the door.

Then he heard his favorite
person walk across the floor.

Sherman began barking and bounded down the stairs.

He ran through the dining room
knocking down the chairs.

Finally he found her,
our family's other guest.

“Sherman! Nice to see you!
You are the best.”

Grandma rubbed his belly.
She scratched behind his ears.

“What a good dog you are.
Don’t you think so, Dears?”

We all said, "Yes, Grandma," as we rolled our eyes.

Sherman just wagged his tail,
and let out happy sighs.

Sherman was a good dog for the rest of the day.

But we knew what would happen the minute Grandma went away.

When I Am Happy

Written by Frank Christian

Illustrated by Marie Garafano

When I am happy,
I draw pictures.

Sometimes I go
to the park.

I play tag with my friends
or go down the slide.

When I am sad,
Dad tickles me.
It makes me laugh.

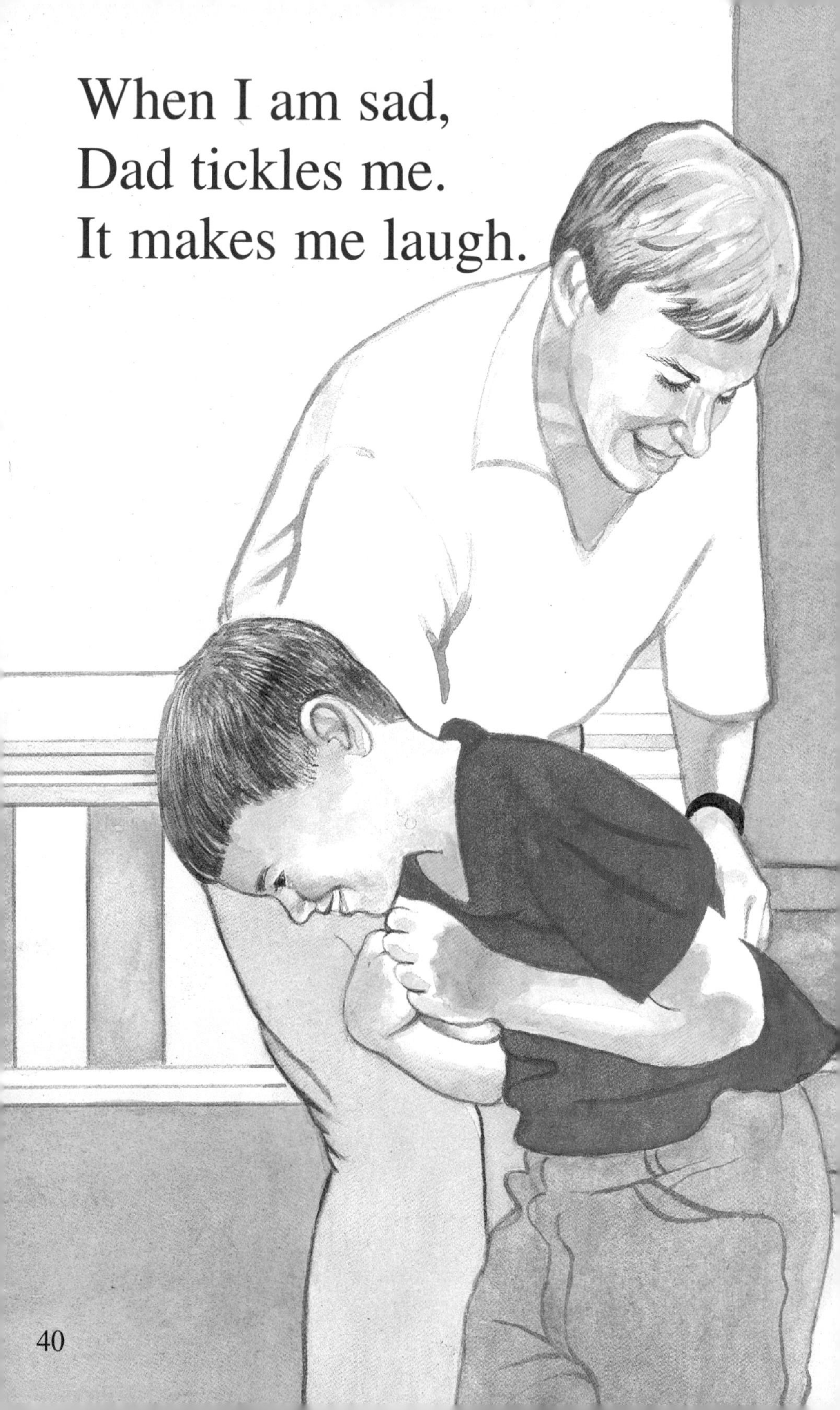

Mom gives me
a kiss and I feel
happy again.

When I am
hungry, I ask
Mom for
a snack.

Sometimes she
gives me a cookie
and an apple.

The apple
is crunchy.

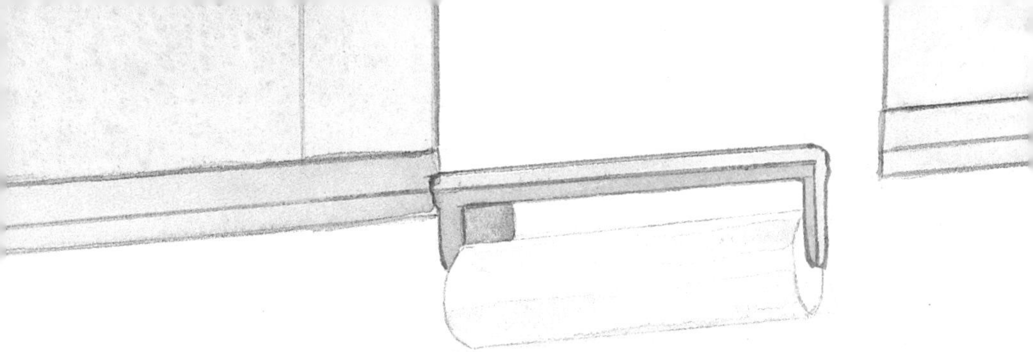

When I am thirsty, Mom
gives me a glass of juice.

When I am
lonely, I help
Mom bake,

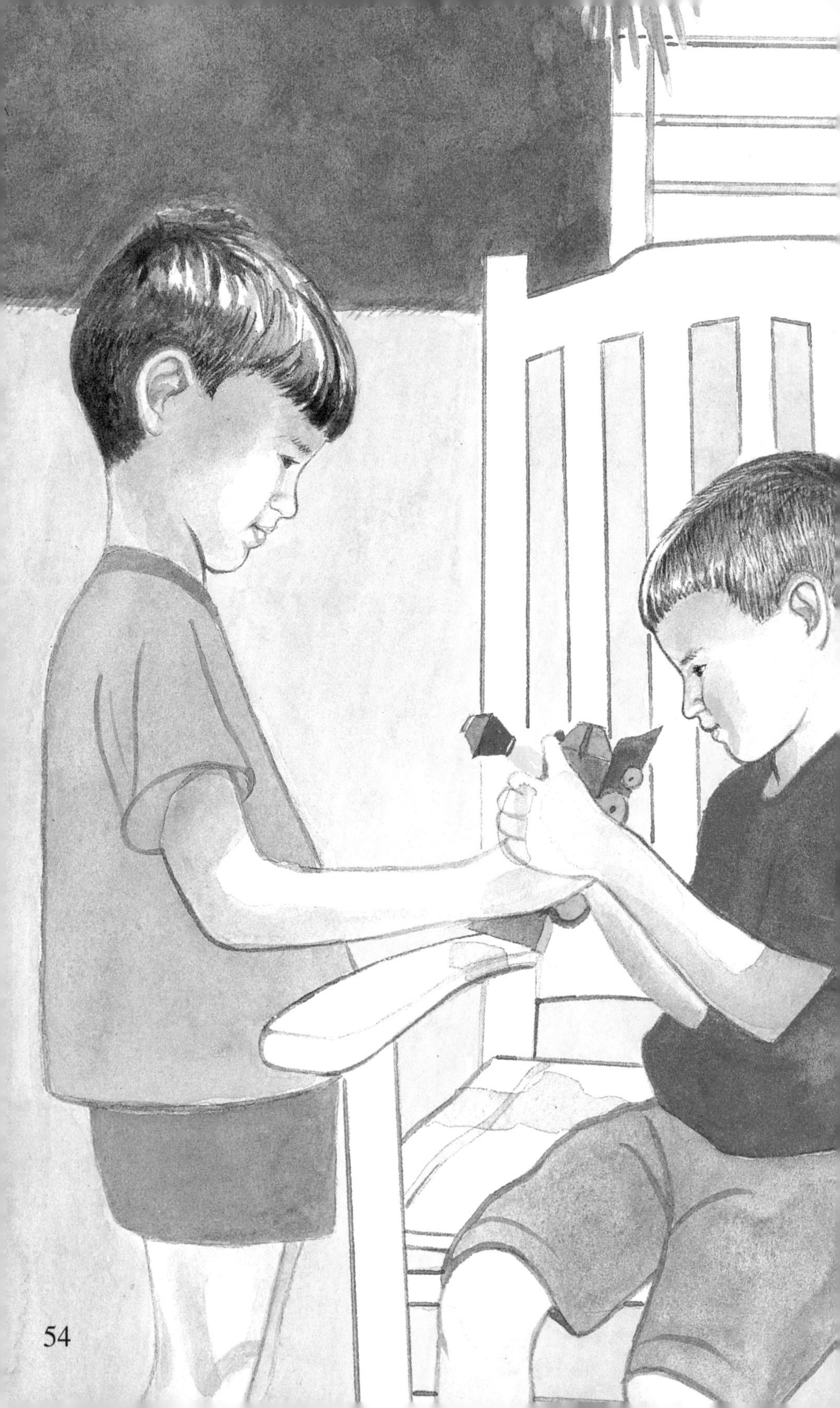

or I go to Jimmy's house.

He shows me his new puppy. The puppy's fur is soft. Its tongue is wet.

When I am hot, Mom takes
me to the pool.

I jump in and the water feels cool.

When I come out, I am wet.

Mom gives me a
towel to dry off.

When I am tired,
I go to bed.

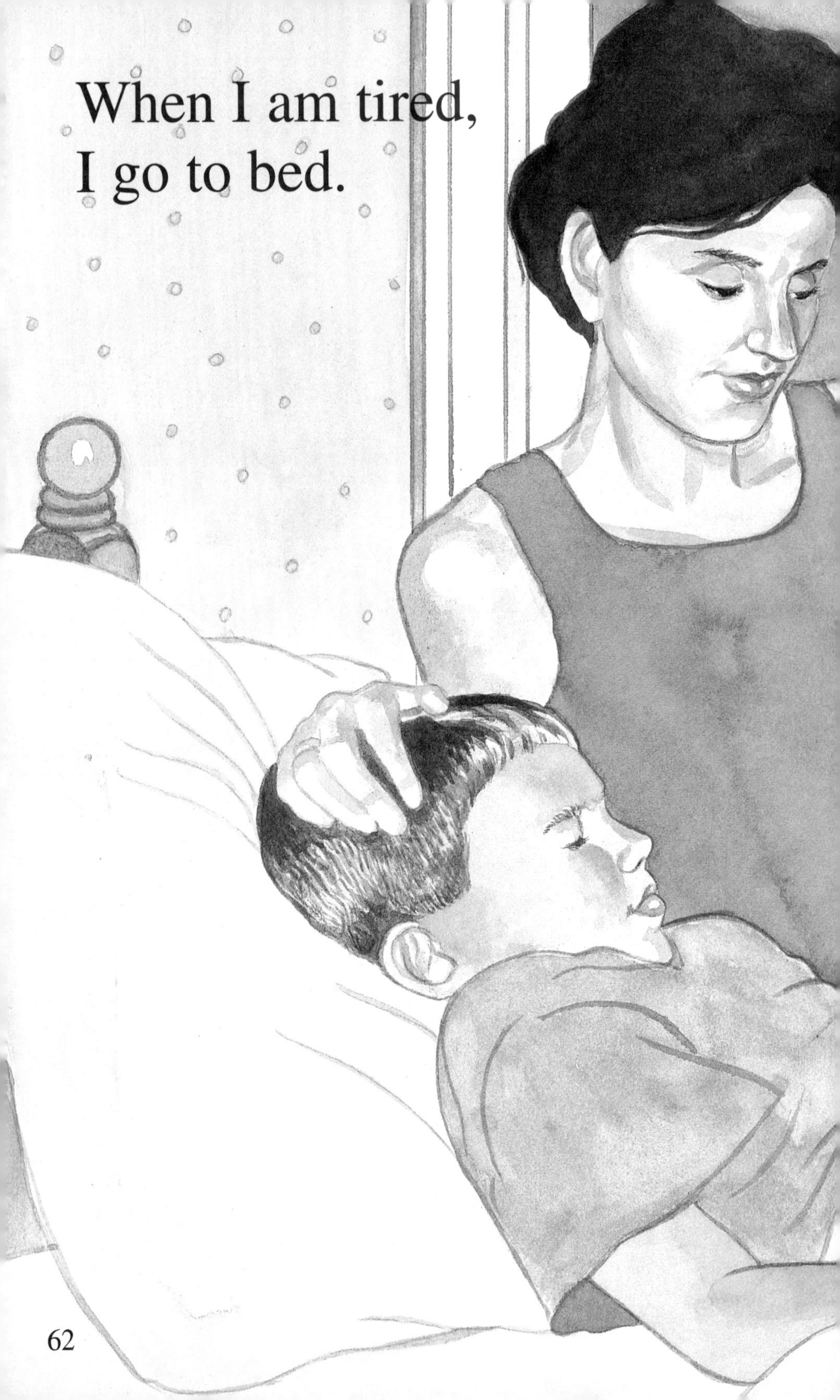

Mom reads me
a story.

Now it is time to
go to sleep.
I am happy.

Treasure Hunting at Tulip Park

Written by R.A. Leslie

Illustrated by Sylvia Ward

Every day Eden Rose and Emma Louise walk to Tulip Park.

One morning Eden Rose says,
"Let's go on a treasure hunt."

At the baseball field, Emma Louise finds a marble.

Can you find the marble in the picture?

At the playground, Eden Rose finds a bell.

Can you find the bell in the picture?

At the skating rink, they find a yo-yo.

Can you find the yo-yo
in the picture?

By the boathouse, Emma Louise finds a toy boat.

Can you find the toy boat in
the picture?

Eden Rose finds a doll
near the lake.

Can you find the doll in the picture?

In the carrot patch, Emma Louise finds a locket.

Can you find the locket in the picture?

At the juice stand, Eden Rose finds a toy car. Emma Louise finds a ring.

Can you find the car and
the ring in the picture?

At the wishing well, they find a coin.
Can you find the coin in the picture?

Now they are back where they started.

"We were treasure hunting,"
Eden Rose tells their friends.
"What did you find?"
Tammy Lynn says.

Eden Rose and Emma Louise look at each other and smile.

“Something for everyone,”
they say together.

Robby gets the marble.
Jean Ann gets the bell.

Tammy Lynn gets the yo-yo.
Christopher gets the boat.

Leo gets the toy car.
Robin gets the ring.

Eden Rose gets the locket.
Emma Louise gets the doll.

With the coin, they buy ice-cream cones for everyone.

Now it is time to go home.

Eden Rose and Emma Louise are happy. They have the best treasure of all—good friends, and each other.

No More Chores!

Written by Andrea Vuocolo

Illustrated by Tim Davis

"Come on, chicks, there are chores awaiting.

There's work to do, so no more playing."

"Mama, dear, we want some fun.

Make a game for everyone."

"Follow me, then, while we clean this place.

I'll put a smile on your face."

"Books are lying across
our track.
Now I guess it's time to
put them back.

Red, orange, yellow,
green and blue,
add some purple and
we'll see a rainbow, too!"

“The dolls and puppets
have had their fun.
It’s back in the toy chest
for every one.

They'll ride this wagon
back to their chest.
Load 'em up chicks, they
need a good rest."

"Some skates, so you can twirl and race. A telescope for outer space.

A ball and mitt for outdoor fun.
A drum and an accordion."

“A jump rope—we can
skip and rhyme.
A puzzle for some
quiet time.

The wagon's loaded
and ready to go.
I think someone is
missing, though."

“Mister Bunny is not
around.
But wait, I think I hear
a sound!”

"Help, I'm lost!"
"Do you hear it too?
Let's go see what we
can do."

"Smooth that sheet, tug
that blanket.
Pull that bedspread—
really yank it.

Out pops Bunny, floppity-flip.
Put him in the wagon, in time
for the trip."

"Let's go, chicks, it's
time to roll,
and join the pet and
plant patrol.

We will take some seeds
and spread them out.
And dig and prune and
give a shout."

“Back inside to feed
the fish.
Look at their colors
and make a wish.

Then tap the fish food,
watch it sink.
I guess HE doesn't
need a drink!"

“The plants get water, so they’ll grow.
It always makes me wonder, though.

It isn't tasty, doesn't crunch.
Is it a bath, or is it lunch?"

"And here we are, at
our last stop.
So circle 'round the
tabletop.

Here are some plates, some forks and some spoons. Dear chicks, take your seats and we'll sing some tunes."

"The books are in order, the
toys put away.
Our pets and plants cared
for—we've had quite a day!

The table is set, so please
take a seat.
Pass me your bowls. It's time
for a treat!"

Colors for Me and You

Written by Frank Christian

Illustrated by Sue Mills

Colors are fun, and isn't it true?

We all have a favorite—how about you?

Jane's dresses have blue polka dots.

Her ribbons are dotted and
so are her socks.

Tim's room has green frogs, a desk and a chair,

a rug, a lamp and even a
green bear!

Tim's glasses make things look green.

Jane's make things blue
when they are seen.

Mike has an orange for his snack. He puts his orange in an orange sack.

After school, Mike and Tim ride their bikes.

At the park, they fly colorful kites.

Sandy likes cherries. They are red and sweet.

The kids play with her
after their treat.

Sandy picks red crayons to use in art class.

Jane puts blue ones in
a blue glass.

Henry juggles balls that are shiny and brown.

Henry is funny and acts
like a clown.

At the farm, Henry rides a brown horse.

Mike likes the orange butterflies, of course.

Sue goes to the circus with her friend Sandy.

Sue bought some yummy pink cotton candy.

Sue helps her mother make icing for a cake.

Her friends are there to
help them bake.

The yellow flowers make Tom sneeze.

Mike picks orange daisies
and watches the bees.

We all have a favorite color—

Jane and Mike, Sandy and Tim, Henry and Tom, let's not forget Sue.

Which of these colors is the color for you?

Ed Can Help

Written by Sallianne Norelli

Illustrated by Diana Zourelias

Now that Ed is six, he can help at home.

Ed likes to help.

Ed helps his dad look for the car key.

After they find it, they go out for ice cream!

Ed's mom likes to work in the garden.

Ed helps her pull
the weeds.

Ed helps his mom
plant flowers.

The flowers are pretty.

Ed helps his sister Elsie write the alphabet.

Elsie is learning fast.

Ed shows his brother Edgar how to tie shoelaces.

Ed rakes leaves with the neighbor, Mr. Wells.

Then they play catch
in the yard.

Ed and Elsie carry the
newspapers outside.
"Here comes the
truck," Elsie says.

Ed doesn't like to clean his room, but Elsie helps him.

Then Ed and Elsie have time to play.

GLUE

At school, Ed and Ray clean the paintbrushes.

Ed's sister Ellen helps
him with his homework.
They work on math.

2+1=3

Everyone helps
set the table for
dinner.

Ed puts out the plates.
Edgar and Elsie fold
the napkins.

Ellen helps bake a cake.
The frosting tastes yummy.

In Ed's family, everyone has a job to do.

Now that Ed is six,
he can help a lot!

Look at Lisa Go

Written by C. Louise March

Illustrated by Gemma Page

Lisa likes to ride her bike on a sunny day.

Lisa rides to the park
where she likes to play.

Lisa can skate around and around the park rink.

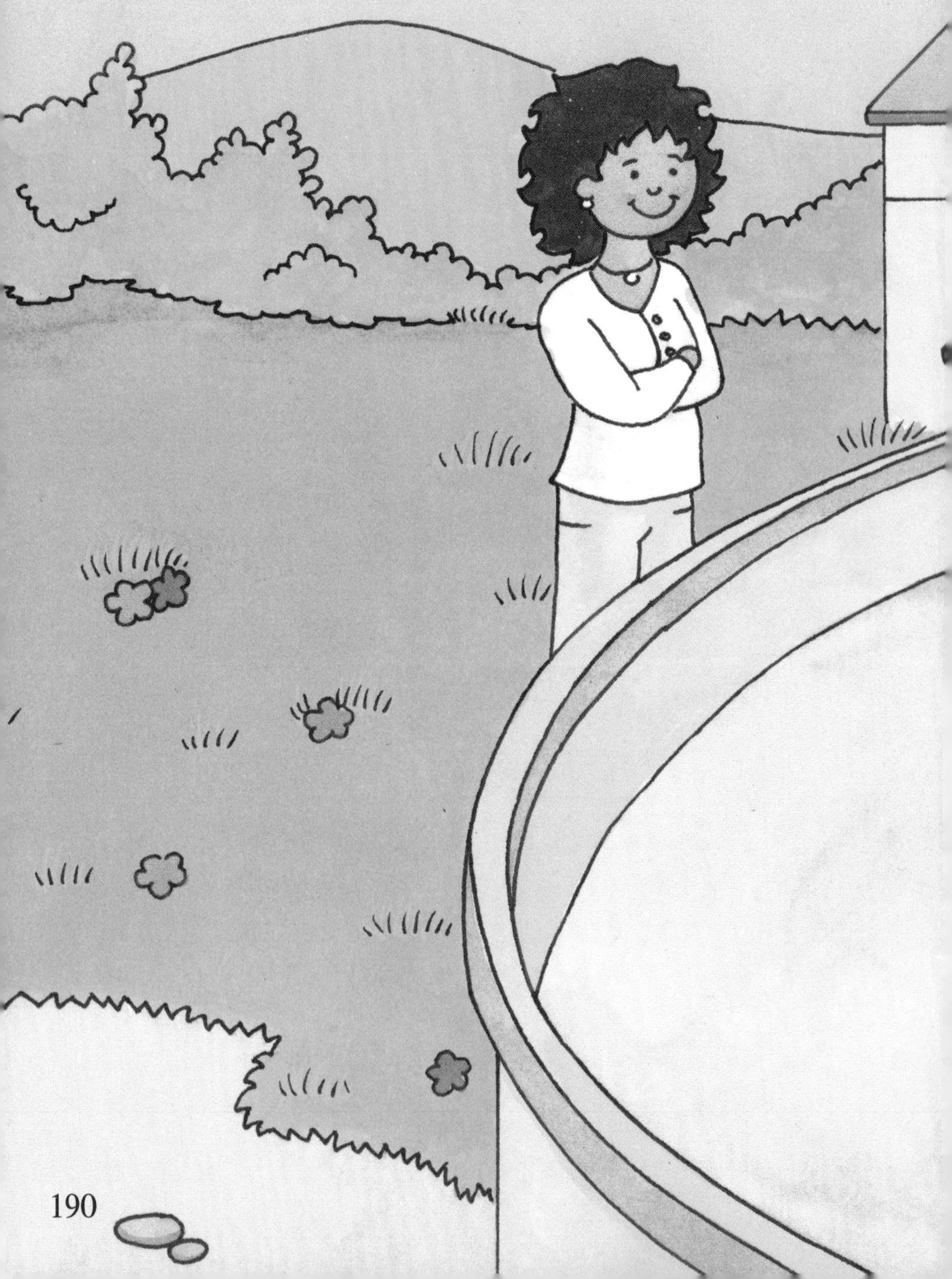

Her skates have new laces
that are bright pink.

Lisa rides a scooter to her friend's pool.

Nick waves hello and says,
"You look cool."

Lisa's friend Tess says
to drive her toy car.

“Look at me,” Lisa says.
“I can go far.”

In winter, Lisa slides down a big hill.

Lisa shows her sled to her friend Jill.

Lisa gets a skateboard from her mom and dad.

Riding the skateboard
makes Lisa glad.

Lisa likes to move fast—
walking is too slow.

Everyone who knows her says,

"Look at Lisa go!"

Goldi's Locks

Written by Harriet Lesser

Illustrated by Arthur A. Davis

One day Goldi wanted to visit her friends, the Three Bears.

But when she woke up,
her hair was a mess.

It was knotted and tangled and worst of all wild.

So she put on her mother's new hat to cover it up.

The Three Bears were happy to see Goldi again.

"Take off your hat and stay a while," they said. "We'll have tea and cookies."

When Goldi pulled off her hat,
the Bears were surprised.

"What happened, Goldi?"
Mama Bear asked.
"Your hair is knotted and tangled
and worst of all wild!"

"I brushed it. I combed it. Nothing helped!" she sobbed. "Did you wash it, Goldi?" Mama Bear asked.

"No. The shampoo makes my eyes sting," Goldi said.

"I can help," said Papa Bear. He tried to pull Goldi's hair into a ponytail.

But it was still knotted and tangled and worst of all wild.

"I can help," said Mama Bear, and she tried to braid Goldi's hair.

But it was still knotted and tangled and worst of all wild.

Mama Bear and Papa Bear looked at each other. They took bunches of Goldi's hair and made pigtails.

“Ouch,” Goldi cried.
It looked awful.

"We can help," Mama and Papa Bear said together.

They wrapped
Goldi's hair into
a beehive hair-do.

"I can help," said
Baby Bear.

He handed Goldi a bottle of
Mrs. Bee's No Sting Shampoo.

Mama Bear washed Goldi's hair.

There were lots of suds
but they didn't sting
Goldi's eyes.

The Bears combed and brushed Goldi's hair.

It had no knots
or tangles.

Mrs. Bee's shampoo worked! Goldi's locks were no longer knotted and tangled. Her hair was shiny and neat.

Goldi looked in
the mirror.
She smiled.

Mama Bear served tea and cookies.

"Thank you for helping me," Goldi said.

After tea, Goldi said good-bye.
"Wait," Baby Bear said.
"I have something for you."
Goldi smiled. It was just
what she needed.

My Friend Nelly

Written by Wendy Gelsanliter

Illustrated by Rosa Guimarães

My friend Nelly lives next door.

I go with her to the grocery store.

Nelly buys food for her dog, Billy.

I buy a bone for my dog, Willy.

Billy and Willy have lots of fun.

They run and jump and
lie in the sun.

Sally comes over with her dog, Corey.

"Hi, Nelly," she says,
"Tell us a story."

Nelly sits down in her old rocking chair,

and tells us about when
she went to the fair.

When Nelly was our age,
she rode the Ferris wheel.

Stopping at the top always made her squeal!

Nelly likes to cook
and so do we.

We make an apple pie
to have with tea.

Sammy comes over with
his pet snail.

"Hi Nelly," he says,
"Tell us a tale."

Nelly says once she rode a polka dot horse.

I say, "You're kidding!"
Nelly says, "Of course."

She tells us about her
real pet snake.

His skin was lots of colors
and his name was Blake.

Nelly works in the garden,
pulling up weeds.

We all help her and feed
the birds seeds.

Lucy comes over with
her big blue bird.

“Tell us a joke, Nelly,
one we’ve never heard.”

Nelly tells a good joke
that makes us all laugh.

It's the joke about the
singing and dancing giraffe.

The sun begins to set in the big blue sky.

Sally, Sammy and Lucy
say good-bye.

The day has now come to an end. I'm so happy that Nelly is my friend.

Sara's Secret Hiding Place

Written by C. Louise March

Illustrated by Art Mawhinney

Sara has three brothers.
They like to play with her.

When Sara wants to play alone,
she goes to her tree house.

"Where's Sara?" Donny asks.

"In her tree house," Keith says.

Donny misses Sara.

"Sara, can I come up?"
Donny asks.

"No," Sara says. "I'm fighting a dragon."

“I can fight a dragon,”
Donny says.

Sara and Donny fight the dragon.

“Where’s Sara?” Johnny asks.

"In her tree house," Keith says.

Johnny misses Sara.

"Sara, can I come up?"
Johnny asks.

“No, Sara says. “We’re playing pirates.”

"I can be a pirate," Johnny says.

Sara and her brothers find buried treasure.

"Where's Sara?" her mom asks.

“In her tree house” Keith says.

Keith misses Sara.

“Sara, can I come up?” he asks.

“No,” Sara says. “We’re digging in Egypt.”

“I can dig, too,” Keith says.

Sara and her brothers find dinosaur bones.

O

“Can we come back tomorrow?” Keith asks. “We can play cowboys!” Johnny says.

Sara nods. She wants to
play cowboys.

Sara likes playing with her brothers after all.